# A New Script for Streamlined Lettering

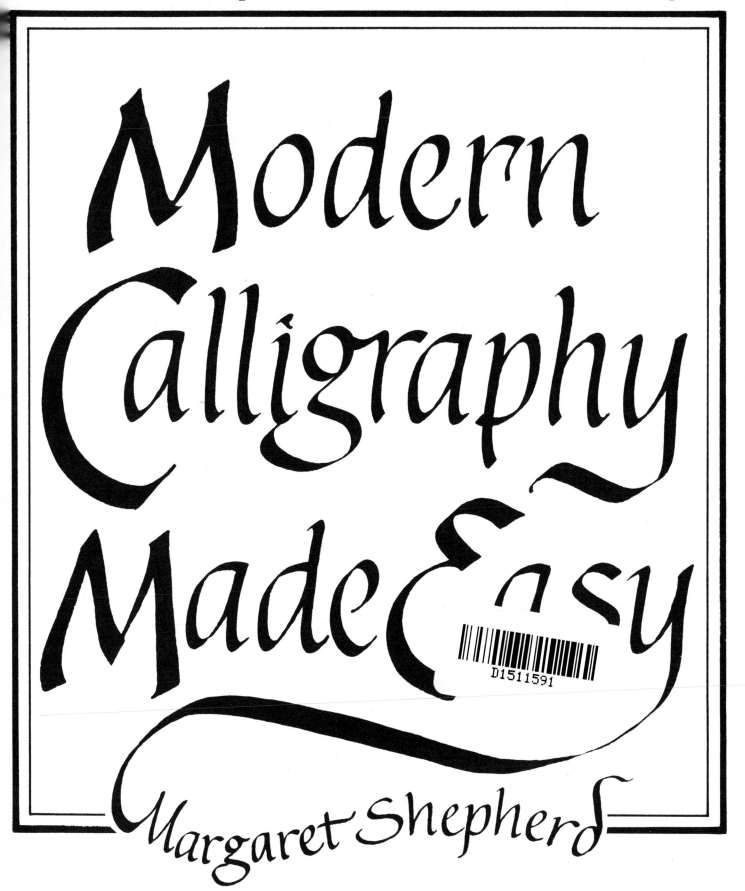

# Modern Calligraphy Made Easy

Margaret Shepherd

Author of CALLIGRAPHY MADE EASY

A Perigee Book

Perigee Books
are published by
The Putnam
Publishing Group
200 Madison Ave.,
New York, NY 10016

Library of Congress Cataloging-in-Publication Data
Shepherd, Margaret.
    Modern calligraphy made easy.  /Margaret Shepherd
      p.    cm.
    ISBN 0~399~51450~3
    1. Calligraphy.   I. Title.
Z43.S5445 1988    87-29224  CIP
745.6'197—dc19

Printed in the United
States of America
    4 5 6 7 8 9 10

# CONTENTS

OTHER BOOKS BY MARGARET SHEPHERD
Calligraphy Made Easy· A Beginner's Workbook
Calligraphy Projects for Pleasure and Profit
Calligraphy Alphabets Made Easy
Learning Calligraphy· A Book of Lettering, Design, and History
Using Calligraphy· A Workbook of Alphabets, Projects, and Techniques
Borders for Calligraphy· How to Design a Decorated Page
Capitals for Calligraphy· A Sourcebook of Decorative Letters

# Introduction

This book will help you get started in calligraphy if you are a beginner, or strengthen your skills if you already have some experience. Either way you will find that its Fundamental Alphabet simplifies your whole approach to lettering; the explanations are streamlined, the practice sheets are foolproof, and the projects are structured to ensure success.

The Fundamental Alphabet will help your calligraphy not only *be* simpler but also *look* simpler. Every stroke is functional & every letter is harmonious. There are no extra ornaments, serifs, or swashes. The overall effect is one of balance and restraint. It lends itself to many practical uses where the more decorative Italic or Gothic alphabets would seem too antique. Once you are familiar with this alphabet and see how it works in the useful projects provided here, you can begin looking for new things to letter every day. Contemporary calligraphy can supplement your job skills, serve the needs of clubs and organizations, add to your enjoyment of a hobby, brighten family occasions, and help you express your own individual creativity.

Margaret Shepherd

# Materials

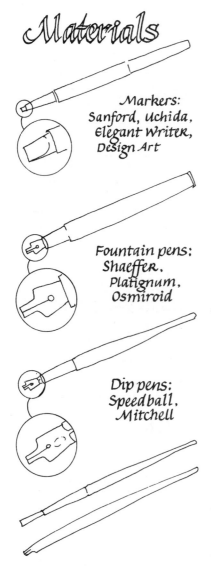

Markers:
Sanford, Uchida,
Elegant Writer,
Design Art

Fountain pens:
Shaeffer,
Platignum,
Osmiroid

Dip pens:
Speedball,
Mitchell

If you cannot find a flat-nibbed pen, or if the marker you have is too wide, you can cut any marker down, as shown here.

There are many calligraphy pens—or, in a pinch, you can make your own. Some of the common brands are shown here at left, with the simplest ones at the top & the more difficult ones at the bottom.

*Markers* come in many widths & colors, some of which will fade in sunlight. *Fountain pens* in various widths can be filled with water-based ink of any color. *Dip pens* are sharper & can be dipped into any liquid that doesn't carry too much pigment; the dipping interrupts your practice repeatedly. *Flat brushes* and *feather quills* can be used with almost any ink or paint.

To get the most out of the exercises & projects in this book, the kind of pen is less important than its width. Make a few strokes in the space at left and compare widths with the sample strokes shown.

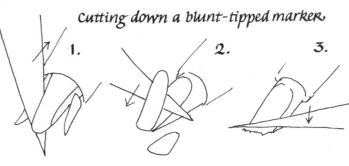

*Cutting down a blunt-tipped marker*

1.                    2.                    3.

# Pen Position & Warmup

To get acquainted with your calligraphy pen, try a few warm-up exercises. Sit in a **straight-backed** chair and lay this book on a flat,*uncluttered desk or table that allows you plenty of room. Your elbow should rest on the surface, not hang over the edge.

Flatten the book open gently using the heel of your hand. Hold it open with your free hand. Your writing hand should hold the pen in the position shown in the drawing here. If you are accustomed to a different way of holding the pen, shift it around until it feels familiar. Then line it up with the pen, not the hand, in the drawing. This is the best pen position for all of the pen strokes and alphabets in this book; check it from time to time to be sure it does not change.

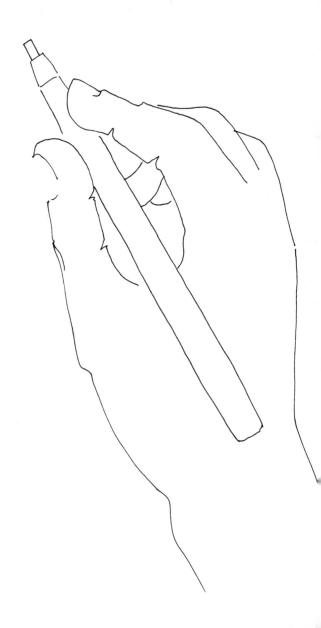

* or slightly inclined.

*Trace gray strokes and then continue on your own with the same stroke pattern.*

Trace the warm-up strokes shown here, keeping the pen position constant. Strive for steady speed and moderate pressure. If you move the pen too slowly and press down too hard, your letter stroke will look rigid, as too much ink may soak in and the pen may tear the surface of the paper. On the other hand, if your pen strokes are quick and light, your letters will look superficial, as the ink edges may appear ragged & tentative. Should you encounter any of these problems, change your pen pressure or speed.

*Too rigid    Blotted ink    Snagged paper     Superficial    Incomplete ink coverage*

*Trace gray strokes and then continue on your own with the same strokes.*

Now you can really get down to basics. Practice the strokes above, over and over. Stop after each completed line and look at it critically. Are the straight strokes really straight, or do they lean? Do the two half-circles add up to one smooth circle? Do the arches appear structurally sound or ready to cave in? Do the diagonals all slant the same amount? Use your eye to analyze your letters so that you don't just grind in your mistakes when you practice.

*Incorrect strokes*

# The Fundamental Alphabet

Now that the calligraphy pen has begun to feel familiar in your hand, you can learn the Fundamental Alphabet with it. These letters are built on the familiar alphabet that every child learns in first grade, that daily meets your eye in newspapers & books, and that you are reading in this book. It combines circles, straight lines, diagonals, & arches to form simple, beautiful shapes while the nib varies the strokes from thick to thin, and finishes off each main stroke with a small *serif.*

I O n V

4 Basic shapes

Check your pen position against the drawing on page 5; then practice the 4 basic shapes until they are familiar.

IIIIII                    OOO

Trace and copy

nnn                    VVV

Trace and copy

I I

Watch how the straight strokes end; they bend only a little before the pen moves sideways to make the serif's thin line.

IIIIII

Letter bodies

IIIIII                    Descenders

Ascenders

If you join straight lines to circles, you will get one group of letters. Write them out, noting similarities & differences.

c d o

Round letters: basic strokes

b d p q

Trace and copy

g o a c e

The second group of letters is made of straight lines joined to arches. Some letters are upside-down versions of others.

n

Basic strokes: arched letters

h f j m

Trace and copy

n r s t u

The rest of the letters are made of diagonal and straight strokes. These 3 groups form the Fundamental Alphabet.

i v

Basic strokes: diagonal letters

l k i w

Trace and copy

v x y z

Practice the Fundamental Alphabet on pages 13 through 26 by lettering over the pale gray guide letters on the first two lines and then copying the Model Letter on the next two lines. If you need to make additional practice paper, use one of the following methods:

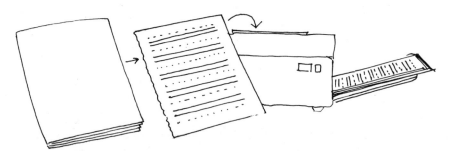

1. Pull, tear, or cut paper out of book. Use copy machine to run multiple copies...

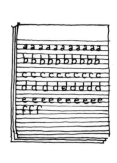

2. ...or lay thin bond paper over it so that the lines show through faintly. (Don't use tracing paper; the ink won't soak in properly.

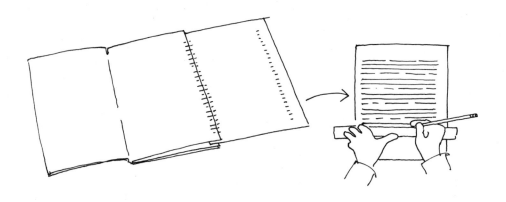

3. If page is missing, or you don't want to remove it, measure ⅜" (6mm) along the 2 side margins of a blank sheet of paper with a ruler, or use the right edge of this page...

... and connect the dots with a ruler or straightedge. Skip every third one, so as to leave plenty of space.

4. Buy a pad or notebook with widely spaced blue lines. Letter in every third line, leaving 2 lines between.

a

*upper right-hand corner is rounded, not square.*

Trace

Trace and copy

Trace and copy

Copy

a

*An alternate letter. Arch the first stroke, then form a compressed loop with the second.*

Trace

Trace and copy

Trace and copy

Copy

1

2

b b b b b b b

Trace

b

Trace and copy

b

Trace and copy

b

Copy

*Lower left-hand corner is rounded, not square.*

2

1

C C C C C C C

Trace

C

Trace and copy

C

Trace and copy

C

Copy

*C is like an incomplete O.*

d d d d d d d
Trace

d
Trace and copy

d
Trace and copy

Second stroke overlaps third
stroke (arrow).

d
Copy

e e e e e e e e
Trace

e
Trace and copy

e
Trace and copy

Center stroke of E slants up.

e
Copy

**f**

Cross-stroke of f is longer on right-hand side.

f f f f f f f f f
Trace

f
Trace and copy

f
Trace and copy

f
Copy

**g**

Upper right-hand corner is rounded, not square.

g g g g g g g
Trace

g
Trace and copy

g
Trace and copy

g
Copy

g

Trace

Trace and copy

Trace and copy

An alternate
G. Outside of top
part fits inside
lower part.

Copy

h

Trace

Trace and copy

Trace and copy

Copy

Trace

Trace and copy

Trace and copy

Copy

*Dot the I and J (below)*
*with a flattened rectangular*
*stroke.*

Trace

Trace and copy

Trace and copy

Copy

*1*

*2*

*3*

*Second stroke intersects first below center; third intersects second above center.*

k k k k k k

Trace

k

Trace and copy

k

Trace and copy

k

Copy

l l l l l l l l l l l l

Trace

l

Trace and copy

l

Trace and copy

l

Copy

m

1    2    3

*M's arches are narrower than N's.*

m m m m m m

Trace

m

Trace and copy

m

Trace and copy

m

Copy

n

1    2

n n n n n n

Trace

n

Trace and copy

n

Trace and copy

n

Copy

O

Trace

Trace and copy

Trace and copy

Copy

P

Third stroke overlaps first.

Trace

Trace and copy

Trace and copy

Copy

q

*Upper right-hand corner is rounded, not square.*

Trace

Trace and copy

Trace and copy

Copy

r

*R is like an incomplete N.*

Trace

Trace and copy

Trace and copy

Copy

Visualize S inside O.

S S S S S S S
Trace

S
Trace and copy

S
Trace and copy

S
Copy

The cross stroke is longer on the right-hand side.

t t t t t t t t t
Trace

t
Trace and copy

t
Trace and copy

t
Copy

u

1   2

Trace

Trace and copy

Trace and copy

Copy

v

1   2

Overlap strokes precisely
(arrow).

Trace

Trace and copy

Trace and copy

Copy

W

Trace

Trace and copy

Trace and copy

Copy

X

Trace

Trace and copy

Trace and copy

Copy

Y

1    2

*Second stroke overlaps first (arrow).*

Trace

Trace and copy

Trace and copy

Copy

Z

1

2

3

Trace

Trace and copy

Trace and copy

Copy

ooii

*Correct spacing*

With 26 letters of the Fundamental Alphabet under your belt, you can begin to form words. The spacing will depend on the *area*, not the *distance*, between letters. Practice combinations.

ooii

*Incorrect spacing*

ata                          crc

*Trace and copy*

oiio                          ero

*Trace and copy*

vyo                          yxo

*Trace and copy*

lxo                          mvi

*Trace and copy*

.,;:-"?!

*Trace*

To complete your alphabet, practice these punctuation marks. Don't allow them to compete with the letters!

*Trace and copy*

" " " "       ???       !!!!

*Trace and copy*

## Project One: A Sentence

You have a lot to think about now while you letter: holding the pen, forming the letters, controlling the shape of the serif, & keeping the letters evenly spaced. Your first calligraphy project is geared to this state of mind. It's challenging enough to learn from yet structured to assure you of success at the end of the process.

Of all those

arts in which

the wise excel,

Nature's chief

masterpiece

is writing well.

Letter the quotation shown here, first for practice at left, and again on the facing page, tracing over the gray preprinted letters. Color the border and capitals with paint, colored pencils, ink, or markers. If you remove the page from the book, you can frame and hang it for encouragement.

John Sheffield
Duke of Buckinghamshire

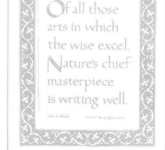

Of all those
arts in which
the wise excel,
Nature's chief
masterpiece
is writing well.

John Sheffield
Duke of Buckinghamshire

# The Fundamental Capitals

Before you go much further with projects that use the Fundamental Alphabet, you will need to learn the Fundamental Capitals. Use them by themselves to letter an entire passage, or capitalize a whole word here & there for emphasis, or just capitalize sentence initials & proper nouns according to normal usage.

Comparative letter height

Capitals, like small letters, are made of a few basic strokes. Practice the letters shown here to get a feel for the main kinds of pen strokes that make up the capital alphabet. Try to make the serifs on the straight ( & diagonal) strokes resemble the serifs on the small letters.

Capitals are taller than the small O, but shorter than the small L—that is, about the same height as the small T. Don't let them tower over the small letters.

Trace and copy:

Straight strokes

Straight and round strokes

Round strokes

Diagonal strokes

Straight and diagonal strokes

IHLT

*Trace and copy*

Vertical & horizontal lines form these letters.

EF

*Trace and copy*

Some straight letters have a slightly curved upper stroke.

OCGQ

*Trace and copy*

These letters follow the path of a circle.

BDPR

*Trace and copy*

Vertical lines join half-circles in these letters.

JSU

*Trace and copy*

Here the half-circles are tops or bottoms of circles.

VWX

*Trace and copy*

These letters are made of diagonal lines.

MNYK

*Trace and copy*

Vertical & diagonal strokes form these letters.

AZ

*Trace and copy*

Horizontal & diagonal lines form these letters.

Now practice each of these letters in greater depth on pages 33 ~ 45, paying attention to similarities and differences.

A

AAAAAA

Trace

A

Trace and copy

A

Trace and copy

A

Trace and copy

ABAB

Trace and copy

B

BBBBBBB

Trace

B

Trace and copy

B

Trace and copy

B

Trace and copy

C 2

1

Trace

Trace and copy

Trace and copy

Trace and copy

Trace and copy

D 1    2

Can be a
separate
stroke.

Lower left-hand corner is
square; upper left-hand
corner is not.

Trace

Trace and copy

Trace and copy

Trace and copy

E E E E E E E E

Trace

E

Trace and copy

E

Trace and copy

Center stroke is a little
shorter than the others.

E

Trace and copy

E

Trace and copy

F F F F F F F

Trace

F

Trace and copy

F

Trace and copy

F

Trace and copy

G

GGGGGG
Trace

G
Trace and copy

G
Trace and copy

G
Trace and copy

*Third stroke is not too long—can be omitted.*

GHGH
Trace and copy

H

HHHHHH
Trace

H
Trace and copy

H
Trace and copy

H
Trace and copy

Trace

Trace and copy

Trace and copy

Trace and copy

Trace and copy

Trace

Trace and copy

Don't start second stroke too high.

Trace and copy

Trace and copy

K

second stroke joins first below center; third joins second above center.

K K K K K

Trace

K

Trace and copy

K

Trace and copy

K

Trace and copy

KLKL

Trace and copy

L

L L L L L L L L L L

Trace

L

Trace and copy

L

Trace and copy

L

Trace and copy

M

MMMM M

Trace

M

Trace and copy

M

Trace and copy

M

Trace and copy

MNM

Trace and copy

N

NNNNN

Trace

N

Trace and copy

N

Trace and copy

Make diagonal center
stroke last.

N

Trace and copy

OOOOOO

Trace

Trace and copy

Trace and copy

Trace and copy

OPOP

Trace and copy

PPPPPPPP

Trace

Trace and copy

Trace and copy

*Third stroke overlaps first.*

Trace and copy

Q Q Q Q Q Q Q

Trace

Q

Trace and copy

Q

Trace and copy

Q

Trace and copy

QRQR

Trace and copy

R R R R R R R

Trace

R

Trace and copy

R

Trace and copy

Keep R's "leg" mostly straight.

R

Trace and copy

S S S S S S S S

Trace

S

Trace and copy

S

Trace and copy

*Visualize a figure 8 when you write S.*

S

Trace and copy

S T S T

Trace and copy

T T T T T T T

Trace

T

Trace and copy

T

Trace and copy

*Top stroke first.*

T

Trace and copy

U

Trace

Trace and copy

Trace and copy

Trace and copy

UVUV

Trace and copy

V

Overlap second stroke
precisely (arrow).

Trace

Trace and copy

Trace and copy

Trace and copy

W

*1   2   3   4*

Each half is narrower
than the V.

Trace

Trace and copy

Trace and copy

Trace and copy

Trace and copy

X

*1   2*

Place second stroke
carefully.

Trace

Trace and copy

Trace and copy

Trace and copy

1

Or: 1

2

3

3

2

*Two different stroke sequences are possible.*

Trace

Trace and copy

Trace and copy

Trace and copy

Trace and copy

Or: 1

1

3

2

3

2

*Two different stroke sequences are possible.*

Trace

Trace and copy

Trace and copy

Trace and copy

# *Project Two: Your Quotation*

The second project builds on what you learned in the first. Instead of tracing over a pre-designed quotation, you will plan, practice, and letter a quotation of your own choosing. Pick a brief passage of prose, a few lines of poetry, a favorite Bible verse, or some words of your own, somewhere between 12 and 15 words in length. Write it in pencil several different ways in the small spaces provided above. Once you find the layout that fits, pen-letter it full-size at left and then recopy it on the bordered page.

# Project Three: Layout

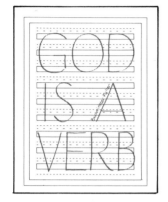

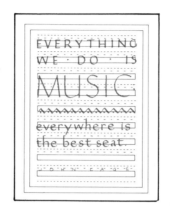

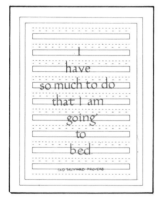

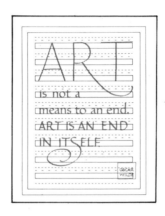

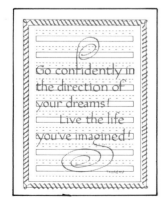

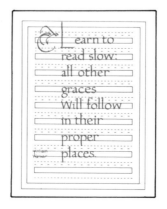

The third project will challenge your growing calligraphy skills, by leaving more decisions up to you. Here are 7 little designs to suggest innovative layouts for any quotation you choose, short or long. On the next page you will find 6 more blank layouts, an alphabet of ornamental capitals, and 3 sections of border that you can copy.

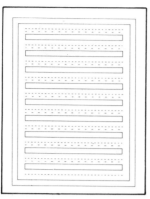
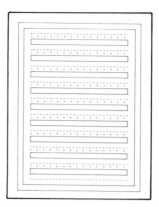
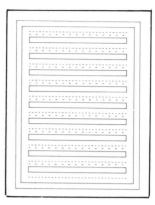

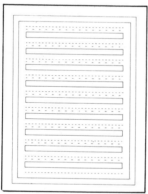
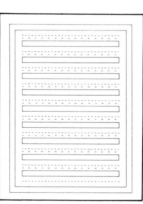
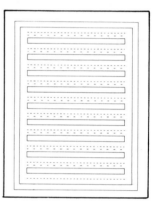

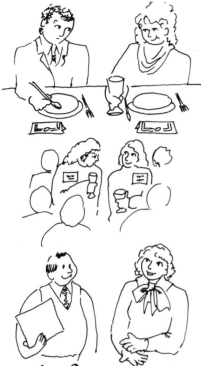

## Project Four: Names

Many calligraphers find that their skills —no matter how precarious—are in great demand. Lettering people's names on diplomas, awards, presentations, place cards, and name badges will not only keep you busy but also polish your skills through repetition. You'll gain mastery of the alphabet while you develop the valuable ability to prevent errors by concentrating.

The fourth project will help you to get right into lettering names, first onto a place card or name badge, and then onto a diploma-style award. The only new skill you must learn is centering (explained on the next page) & then you'll be calligraphically prepared to produce all that's needed for an awards dinner or end-of-year meeting.

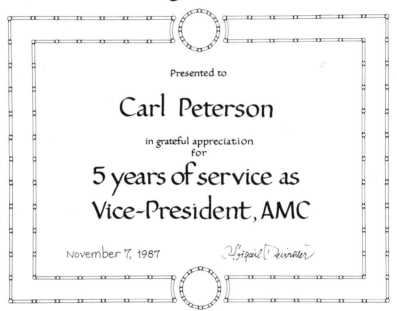

Presented to

**Carl Peterson**

in grateful appreciation
for

**5 years of service as
Vice-President, AMC**

November 7, 1987          Abigail Deirmier

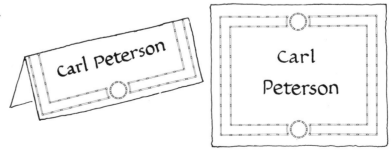

Carl Peterson

Carl
Peterson

To center a name, first write it in the space at left (or use a separate guideline sheet). Then find the mid-point of the name, either by folding it in half, or by measuring it.*
Now position this first draft above the guideline where you will be lettering the name, folding the extra paper out of the way & lining up both center marks. Unfold and repeat for the next name.

Cut the next page into 8 cards. Each is plain on the front, bordered on the back. For name badges, letter name on center line and don't fold. (For first & last names, use place card guidelines.) Attach with pin.

| | |
|---|---|
| Amanda | Amanda |
| Carolyn | Carolyn |
| Christopher | Christopher |
| Maurice | Maurice |

Amanda

Annie    Barbara    Fred Fiske    Michael Aman

* If you don't have a ruler, cut this one off the edge of the page and use it.

7    6    5    4    3    2    1

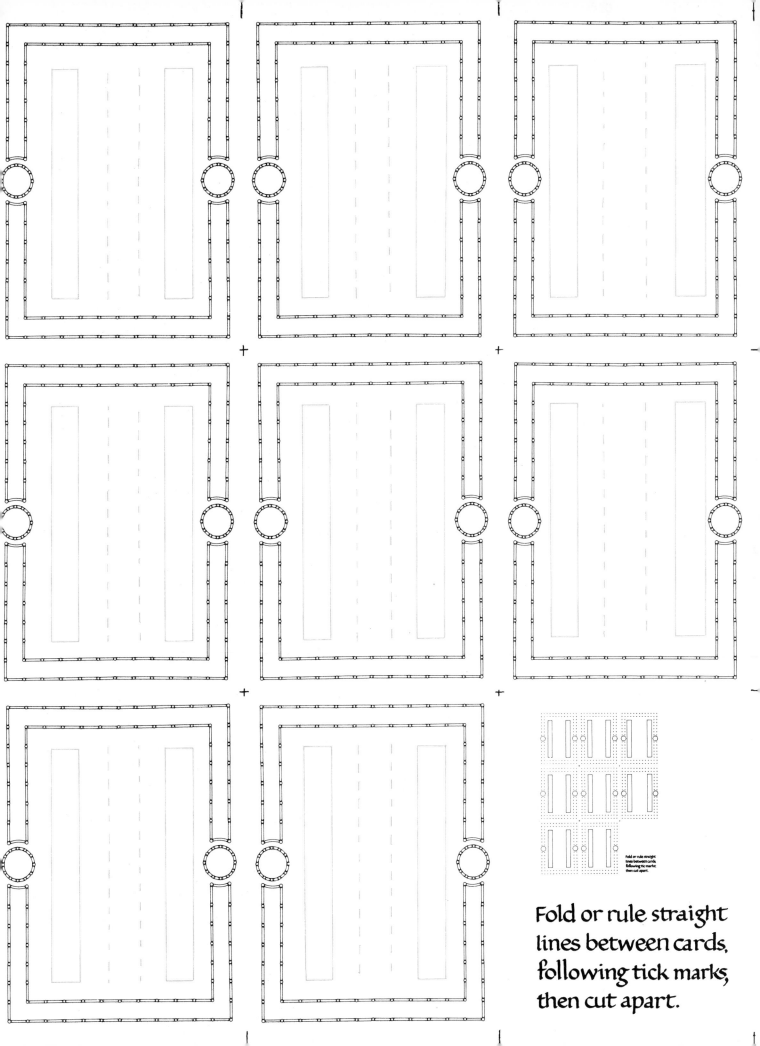

Fold or rule straight
lines between cards,
following tick marks,
then cut apart.

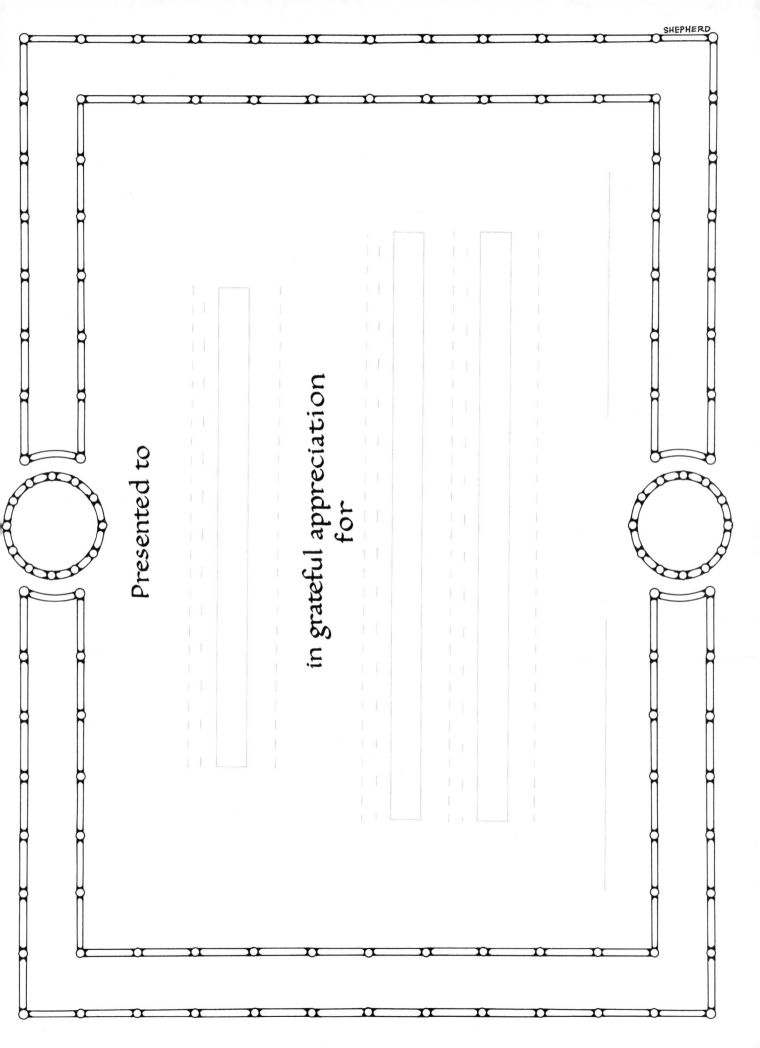

Presented to

in grateful appreciation
for

SHEPHERD

1 1 1 1 1

2 2 2

3 3 3 3

4 4 4

5 5 5 5

## Numerals

One final group of symbols is needed to complete your mastery of the Fundamental Alphabet — numerals. With them, you can letter posters, number seating charts, design stationery, & address envelopes. Practice the first 9 numerals at left, & zero below.

6 6 6 6     0 0

7 7 7 7     0 0

8 8 8 8     0 0

9 9 9 9     0 0

## Project Five: Addresses

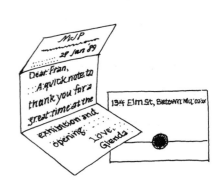

The fifth project is a letter to a friend, a relative, or another calligrapher. The fold-a-note form includes guidelines for your initials and address, date, mailing address, & return address.

207                    783

1349                    9156

58604

Practice numerals in combinations of 3, 4, & 5, spacing them evenly and harmonizing their forms.

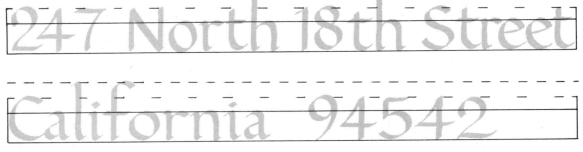

247 North 18th Street

California 94542

Practice numerals also in conjunction with small letters and capitals. They will be the same height as the capitals.

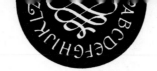

*Stamp*

TO:

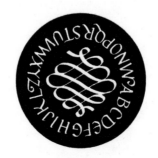